GREAT PICTURES

AND THEIR STORIES

How To Look At Pictures

"You must look at pictures studiously, earnestly, honestly. It will take years before you come to a full appreciation of art; but when at last you have it, you will be possessed of the purest, loftiest and most ennobling pleasures that the civilized world can offer you."

JOHN C. VAN DYKE.

ST.
AA
PRESS

GREAT PICTURES
AND THEIR STORIES

INTERPRETING
MASTERPIECES
TO CHILDREN

BY
KATHERINE MORRIS LESTER

BOOK SIX

ST. AUGUSTINE ACADEMY PRESS

This book was originally published in 1927
by Mentzer, Bush & Company.

This facsimile edition reprinted in 2024
with improved color images
by St. Augustine Academy Press.

ISBN: 978-1-64051-149-1

CONTENTS

Page

The Jester ....*Hals* 13

The Mill ....*Ruysdael* 21

Flower Girl of Holland........*Hitchcock* 33

View of Ghent...............*Baertsoen* 45

A Dutch Interior............*De Hooch*..... 53

Fog Warning ....*Homer* 65

Joan of Arc.................*Bastien-LePage* 73

Joan of Arc................. ....*Chapu* 85

Christ in the Temple..........*Hofmann* 93

The Angelus.................*Millet* 105

INDEX OF ILLUSTRATIONS IN GREAT PICTURES AND THEIR STORIES

BOOK ONE—FIRST GRADE
(All in Color)   Page
1. Baby Stuart................17
2. Nurse and Child............21
3. The Calmady Children.......29
4. Madonna of the Chair.......35
5. With Grandma..............42
6. Children of the Shell........51
7. Princess Margarita Theresia..58
8. Feeding her Birds...........66
9. Children of the Sea..........74
10. The Holy Night.............83

BOOK TWO—SECOND GRADE
(All in Color)   Page
1. A Holiday..................13
2. Mme. Lebrun and Her
      Daughter................21
3. Don Carlos on Horseback....28
4. The Boy With a Rabbit......37
5. The Storage Room.........45
6. The Pastry Eaters..........53
7. The Age of Innocence.......61
8. Home Work................69
9. Children of Charles I.......77
10. Sistine Madonna...........84

BOOK THREE—THIRD GRADE
(All in Color)   Page
1. Miss Bowles...............13
2. Hearing...................20
3. Dancing in a Ring..........29
4. Angel With a Lute..........37
5. An Aristocrat..............45
6. Carnation, Lily, Lily, Rose...53
7. Return to the Fold.........61
8. Pilgrims Going to Church....69
9. Going to Church, Moravia...77
10. The Primitive Sculptor......85

BOOK FOUR—FOURTH GRADE
(All in Color)   Page
1. Aurora....................13
2. The Horse Fair.............25
3. Behind the Plow...........35
4. Venetian Waters...........47
5. The Sheepfold.............59
6. The Gleaners..............69
7. The Solemn Pledge.........81
8. Preparing for Church.......93
9. Going to Market...........103
10. The Blue Boy.............115

BOOK FIVE—FIFTH GRADE
(9 in Color—Statue in Black)   Page
1. Spring Dance...............13
2. After a Summer Shower......25
3. The Sewing School..........33
4. Russian Winter.............41
5. Return of the Fishermen.....49
6. Song of the Lark...........61
7. Santa Fe Trail.............72
8. Appeal to the Great Spirit....81
9. Lady With a Lute...........93
10. Galahad the Deliverer......105

BOOK SIX—SIXTH GRADE
(9 in Color—Statue in Black)   Page
1. The Jester.................13
2. The Mill..................21
3. A Flower Girl of Holland....33
4. View of Ghent.............45
5. A Dutch Interior...........53
6. The Fog Warning...........65
7. Joan of Arc...............73
8. Joan of Arc...............85
9. Christ in the Temple.......93
10. The Angelus..............105

BOOK SEVEN—SEVENTH GRADE
(9 in Color—Statue in Black)   Page
1. Moonlight, Wood's Island
      Light...................13
2. Sir Galahad...............25
3. The Vigil..................37
4. Dance of the Nymphs.......45
5. Icebound..................57
6. The Concert...............65
7. King Cophetua and the
      Beggar Maid............77
8. Frieze of the Prophets (Detail) 89
9. Bartolomeo Colleoni........101
10. Avenue of Trees..........109

BOOK EIGHT—EIGHTH GRADE
(9 in Color—Statue in Black   Page
1. George Washington.........13
2. On the Stairs..............25
3. Cotopaxi.................33
4. Syndics of the Cloth Guild....45
5. The Artist's Mother........57
6. Church at Old Lyme........69
7. The Last Supper...........77
8. St. Genevieve.............89
9. The Fighting Temeraire.....101
10. Victory of Samothrace.....113

BOOK NINE—FOR JR. AND SR. HIGH AND NORMAL SCHOOLS
                          Page
1. James Whitcomb Riley.......10
2. The Mill Pond.............22
3. The Northeaster............30
4. The Whistling Boy..........42
5. Men of the Docks..........54

                          Page
6. The Virgin.................66
7. King Lear.................78
8. Battersea Bridge...........90
9. The Apotheosis of Pittsburgh.102
10. Abraham Lincoln.......... 114

FOREWORD

Picture Study is rapidly becoming an important factor in our public school education. "Nearly every progressive city," says the Bureau of Education, Washington, D. C., "is making use of some form of picture study in the public school system."

The twentieth century has ushered in the reproduction of masterpieces in colors! To what heights of delight the children of the public schools may be carried by the famous pictures of the world in color!

It remains only for the elders to choose pictures adapted to the childish interests; pictures which will cultivate a taste for the best in art; pictures which through the impressionable early years will lead to a true understanding and appreciation of the world's masterpieces!

In preparing this series of readers it has been the aim of those selecting the pictures to consider always the child interest. The field of pictures is large. Not only have the "old masters" been drawn upon, but masters in modern art as well, including modern American artists. Thus constantly, through this series of pictures, the principles of beauty which made possible the "old masters" of yesterday are seen again in the art of today.

In the preparation of the text the child's interest and his ability to read are carefully considered. Real picture knowledge is conveyed in the child's own language.

In the primary grades the interest is largely in "what it is all about." Consequently the text aims to satisfy this curiosity, and at the same time lead to unconscious observation of those things which are most alive to the little child,—color, life, action.

The vocabulary for Books I, II, and III is based on "The Reading Vocabulary," * the Horn, Horn, and Packer List.

*See twenty-fourth Year Book, National Society for the Study of Education, Part I, 1925.

In the intermediate grades, a lively interest in the story is always uppermost. Gradually an appreciation of picture-pattern develops. Simple elements in picture making,—i.e. center of interest, repetition of line and color,—may be intelligently comprehended by children of the intermediate grades.

In the grammar grades great interest in the story continues, and with this interest there develops an appreciation of HOW the story is told,—the real ART of the picture. The pupil not only learns that the picture is a masterpiece, but WHY. He thus acquires standards for judging other pictures.

Each picture is followed by a short sketch of the artist, told in a key adapted to the age and interest of the pupil.

The questions which follow the text will assist in developing an intelligent appreciation of the picture.

The author is particularly indebted to Miss Jennie Long, recently Supervisor of Primary

Education, Peoria Public Schools, for valuable criticism of the primary text. Grateful acknowledgment is also made for the opportunity of practical work with a selected number of primary stories in the schools of Peoria.

The manuscripts of the intermediate and grammar grade books have been submitted to teachers of these grades, to whom the author is indebted for helpful practical suggestions.

The MUSICAL SELECTIONS for the pictures have been graciously contributed by Eva G. Kidder, Director of Music, Peoria Public Schools. The author believes this to be a very valuable feature of these books.

KATHERINE MORRIS LESTER.

ILLUSTRATED WITH REPRO-
DUCTIONS IN COLOR FROM
THE ORIGINAL MASTER-
PIECES, BY COURTESY OF
THE ART EXTENSION
SOCIETY OF NEW YORK.

THE JESTER
Rijksmuseum, Amsterdam

ARTIST: Frans Hals
SCHOOL: Dutch
DATES: 1580-1666

THE JESTER

This gay mischievous fellow is posing for his picture as a "jolly mandolier." He must be serenading beneath a favorite window. He has been twanging the strings of his friendly guitar for some time. Now his eyes catch sight of some one he knows, and a glad smile of recognition spreads over his face.

You will be surprised to know that "the jester" was a well known artist in Holland. His name is Adriaen Brouwer. Many of his pictures hang in the galleries of Europe.

He was a pupil of Frans Hals, and known far and wide for his practical jokes. Among his fellow painters he had earned the nickname, "Funny-man." Away back in sixteen hundred, the artists of Holland had gay good times. They used to meet in the various studios, and sing and play to their hearts' content. Adriaen Brouwer was a genius in music as well as a painter of note. Today he is masquerading in jester's attire. He wears a Spanish jacket trimmed with bands of red. No doubt there are bells on his gay yellow cap. With his loose flowing locks and his cap atilt, he twangs his strings and glances upward. This must be a familiar call to someone who knows it well, for the answer comes, as expected, at the window above.

A smile such as this is only for a moment. In an instant the face changes. Quick must be the artist who would catch and fix upon canvas an expression so fleeting!

The hands, too, must not be forgotten. They mean much in the picture. With a short, crisp note the serenade has just finished. The hands are still in position. They are in perfect tune with the expression of the face. It is as though the jester had posed for an instantaneous photograph.

Notice how the sunlight falls upon

the face and hands. This makes the color here very light, while all else is in shadow. The lighting of the face and two hands helps to emphasize the three spots in the picture. The three combine as one to express the gay happy mood of the jester.

This is considered the finest "expression" portrait in the world. It is called by many names,—"The Jester," "The Jolly Mandolier," and "The Fool with a Lute." We may choose the name we like best.

THE ARTIST

Frans Hals, the Dutch painter, was a friend of the jolly mandolier. Indeed it was Hals who discovered Brouwer's great genius as a painter. When a young lad he became a pupil of Hals. He was a kind of "happy go lucky" fellow, naturally gifted, but not applying himself. It is said that Hals, to keep him at work, shut him up in a garret and forced him to paint many small pictures each day. These Hals purchased at a penny each, and resold at a handsome profit. Poor Brouwer soon decided to break away from Hals and go to Amsterdam. He arrived in Amsterdam penniless, but not discouraged. His first picture sold for one hundred ducatoons.* The story says that Brouwer was dumbfounded by such an enormous sum. He ran home with his bag of gold, emptied it out on the floor, and then rolled himself back and forth over it several times. Then he gathered it up, and inside of ten days it was spent. "Thank God I have gotten rid of that!" said he; "I feel all the lighter for it."

No doubt Brouwer, later on, spent much of his time in Haarlem at the studio of Hals, which was a gathering place for all the painters of the town.

Hals was born in Antwerp about the year 1584. For nearly three hundred

---

*A ducatoon equals $1.20; one-half a gold ducat.

years before, the family name, Hals, had been known in Haarlem. Long before Frans was born his ancestors had been of importance and prominence in the little town. By and by, however, during the Dutch and Spanish wars, (1572), the Spanish soldiers attacked and pillaged the town of Haarlem, and forced the Dutch to leave the city.

The elder Hals was among those who took refuge in Antwerp, not far distant. Here Frans Hals was born. By the time he was twenty the family had moved back to Haarlem, and it was here that Frans continued to live, and here he grew to fame.

Very little is known about the life of young Hals, but he probably worked with other painters who were studying in Haarlem. His first pictures are dated 1613 and 1614. As he became more and more skilled in his art, he was in great demand for portraits, for everybody in Holland was eager to have his portrait painted. There were no great lords and ladies living in this little town of Haarlem, so the artists had to content themselves by painting the people about them. Hals painted no beauties, but his pictures are full of interest.

Frans Hals is the most successful painter of a smile that we know. His portraits are always smiling, singing, or playing upon musical instruments. So fascinating to him was the study of faces, that he often invited friends to his studio, and there entertained them by telling funny stories. Then, in an instant, he would dash off their smiling faces.

Today after three hundred years he still holds his place as one of the great portrait painters of the world.

DIRECTED STUDY

1. Who is the "jester"?
Where did he live? When?
For what is he known?

2. What is the "jester" doing?
   How is he dressed?
   Why does he smile?

3. Where does the sunlight fall?
   In what position are the hands?
   How would relaxed hands change
   the picture?
   Would you like it as well? Why?

4. Why does the picture resemble an
   instantaneous photograph?

5. What is the *art* of the picture?

6. Who is the artist?
   What is an outstanding character-
   istic of all his pictures?
   How does he rank as a painter?
   Where is this picture?

Related Music: LA MANDOLINATA....
.................*Paladilke*
MANDOLIN SONG......
.........*Spanish Folk Song*
LE SECRET—Intermezzo
.... *Gautier*
ROBINS M'AIME......
.............*Troubadour*

THE MILL
Rijksmuseum, Amsterdam

ARTIST: Jacob van Ruysdael
SCHOOL: Dutch
DATES: 1628-1682

THE MILL

A windmill such as this can suggest only one country in the world. That country is Holland. In this low flat country of the Netherlands, the picturesque windmills, with their great arms dot the landscape. Windmills are everywhere in Holland.

Not all windmills, however, are as large as the one in our picture. No doubt the artist chose this mill and its setting with great care. See how its outline and great arms are silhouetted against the moving clouds.

Yes, indeed, the clouds are moving! They are rapidly forming. Their great, soft masses are rolling up against the sky. They reflect a strange light that means storm.

One cloud throws a dark shadow over the point of land. It shadows the water, too. Through a rift in the cloud the sinking sun sends a soft light over the scene. It catches the old mill with its golden glow. It lights up the water, too. It plays along the tall piles, and the three figures above. It lights up the red roof of the little house. The whole scene is mellowed in the fading yellow light. All but the clouds is quiet and still. This is the calm that precedes the storm.

The tall grasses in the foreground are beginning to bend, and the water begins to ripple. Farther out the water is calm and still. It stretches out of sight around the curve of the distant shore. The little boat with its sail is quiet and undisturbed. Its perfect reflection in the water shows the stillness of the air just before the storm breaks.

See the fine distance the artist has given the picture! With a low, low skyline, he has made the distance lead far away. Many times an artist gives distance to his pictures by placing the skyline high, but this painter has done the very opposite. He has placed the skyline very low on the canvas.

How does the artist carry us back so far into the picture? How does he create the illusion of distance? Ah! The painter thought much about this.

See the irregular shoreline! It is a long, long way back when the eye sweeps the deep curves of the inlets—one, two, three—and on to the far horizon. The little sailing boat, too, helps to make the distance seem far away.

The great mass of moving cloud fills two-thirds of the canvas. This gives tremendous force to the coming storm. It is, you see, in marked contrast to the lull on the land and water. It was this moment, just before the storm broke, that the artist caught and fixed upon canvas.

What is it that makes the earth so quiet and still? If you look closely you will see that the artist allows nothing to move but the bending grass in the forefront of the picture.

The sails of the little boat are tall

and straight. They are repeated in the vertical shadows in the water beneath. The two masts of the moored schooner are tall and straight. These tall straight lines are echoed in the vertical piles of the breakwater, especially those in the forefront of the picture, and the shining figures on the land. Tall vertical lines combined with broad horizontal masses always give quietness and repose to a picture. So these vertical accents with the long horizontal mass of land, the hull of the little boat, and the shadow on the water, keep the earth in a quiet lull just as the artist intended.

The grand old mill stands out majestically against the threatening sky. Though it is built upon the ground it towers so high!

Its tall vertical mass seems to hold together the sky and the ground. This gives unity and completeness to the picture. The great oblique arms of the mill do much to break the stillness.

See! They are beginning to swing! Yes, slowly at first, but soon the whole scene will be whipped into movement!

THE STORY OF THE ARTIST

Jacob Ruysdael is today recognized as one of the great landscape painters of the world. Though he is famous as a painter, little is known of his life.

We do know, however, that he was born in Haarlem, Holland, in 1628 or 1629. His father and uncle were picture-dealers and artists. No doubt they were the first to instruct the little Dutch boy in his early efforts to draw.

It is said that the father had hoped to have his son become a physician. Upon discovering, however, his great ability in drawing, which was shown at a very early age, he gave up his cherished plan. He decided that the boy must develop his talent. At the age of twelve years, it is said, the lad had produced pictures that astonished both artists and amateurs alike.

Aside from this we scarcely hear of young Ruysdael until he was nineteen. He was then old enough to enter the guild of painters at Haarlem. At this time a number of young painters were studying here. Later many of the group attained success and fame in Dutch art.

Among the painters who studied with Ruysdael at this time was Meindert Hobbema, who painted "Avenue Middleharnis," and Frans Hals, one of the greatest portrait painters of the world.

Though most of the students of this day were painting figures and interiors in beautiful color, Ruysdael devoted himself to landscape.

You will be surprised to know that Holland was the first country to begin landscape painting. Before Ruysdael's day very few pictures of the great out-of-doors were painted. The first landscapes date back about one hundred years before his time. Previous to that time and down to his own day, landscape was usually painted only as a scenic background for figures. No painter ever tried to make it attractive in itself. Our picture, "The Mill," represents one of the early types of landscape painting. In that day the artists aimed to produce an exact copy of nature. They mixed their colors to secure the effects they saw in nature.

Today an artist more frequently aims to produce his *impressions* of a scene, rather than an exact reproduction of it. Today many artists paint with little spots of pure color placed side by side, instead of mixing colors. This often gives just the effect that the artist wishes.

Unlike most of the painters of his day, Ruysdael found the mountains, moving clouds, trees, and streams of great interest. None could surpass him in representing wind-blown trees, moving water, cascades, or mountain torrents. With all his skill in landscape, however, he was unable to draw figures of men or animals. Consequently, whenever a figure was needed to complete his picture, it was necessary to call upon his fellow artists. Many of them are known to have helped out the painter by adding figures of both men and animals.

Ruysdael found his greatest joy in the broad expanse of Holland sky, and clouds moving over the far-reaching lowlands. He represented nature as it is, but added much of his own imagination and feeling. He was naturally of a sensitive, dreamy disposition, and we are not surprised that his sympathetic response to nature crept into his pictures.

None of Ruysdael's pictures are lively or gay. There is always a note of melancholy. Someone said that he painted the "gray side of life." Even so, his pictures have a charm that has endured for three hundred years.

Notwithstanding Ruysdael's great ability, his pictures were not appreciated. People did not care for the scenes which they saw everyday about them. They thought Ruysdael was wasting his time. They preferred the pictures of other artists. Consequently the painter had a long hard struggle with poverty.

As an old man he was neglected by his townsmen, and died in utter want in the almshouse of Haarlem.

Now, however, he has come into his own! As is true of so many great artists, Jacob Ruysdael's art was far ahead of the time in which he lived. Though his work won neither fame nor honor during his lifetime, today he is placed among the greatest landscape painters of the world. Now people pay fabulous prices for his paintings. His pictures hang in many of the famous galleries of Europe.

"The Mill," which hangs in the Rijks Museum in Amsterdam, is one of the most imposing and beautiful of all his masterpieces. Reproductions of this celebrated painting hang in many public schools, colleges, and universities throughout the world.

DIRECTED STUDY

1. From what country is this a scene?
   What helps you to recognize it?

2. What do you see first?
   What other objects do you see?

3. From what direction does the light come?

4. What is the time of day?
   How do you know?
   Name the different objects that catch the sunlight.
   Where is the highest light?
   Where is the deepest shadow?
   What causes the shadow on the water?

5. How much of the picture is sky? Foreground?
   How does the artist secure distance?
   How does he give repose and quiet to land and water?

6. What impression do the clouds give?
   Does the windmill help? How?
   What in the foreground suggest coming movement?
   What story has the artist told?

7. What do you like best about the picture? Why?

8. Who is the artist? When did he live?
   What kind of pictures did he paint best?
   How were his pictures received?
   How does he rank today?

Related Music: THE HUNGRY WIND-
MILL ....*Terhune*

THE STORM—Wm. Tell
Overture ....*Rossini*

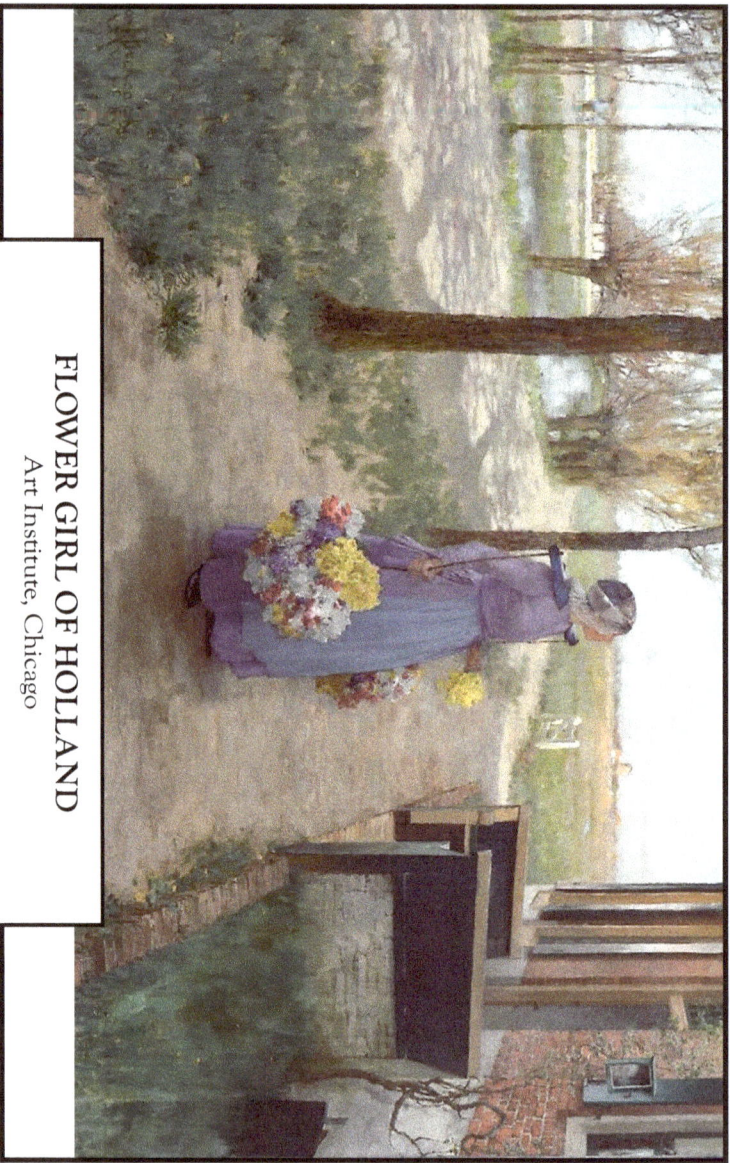

FLOWER GIRL OF HOLLAND

Art Institute, Chicago

ARTIST: George Hitchcock
SCHOOL: American
DATES: 1850-1913

FLOWER GIRL OF HOLLAND

Holland is a quaint little country bordering on the North Sea. It is a land of dikes, canals, and windmills. It is a land of soft green willows and gay-colored flowers.

Any day one may see the happy Dutch girls in their wooden shoes and freshly starched caps, working among their gardens.

And such wondrous gardens they are! Tulips and hyacinths! The gayest in the world! No wonder Holland is known as "Tulip Land"! No wonder the whole world sends to Holland for hyacinth bulbs! With patient care the Dutch fraulein tends her garden. She expects to carry to market the gayest bouquets in all Holland!

Our picture shows the Holland flower girl. She is ready for market. Perhaps, just now, she is stopping at some friendly house to sell her bouquets.

See how she carries her load! The
yoke passes across her shoulders. The
large baskets hang from each end.

What a mass of pretty bright flowers! See the lovely colors! See the
violet dress and blue-green apron!

The artist put shining yellow flowers
against the purple dress. The artist
knew that they are always beautiful
side by side. With her gay bright flowers and her pretty dress she makes a
charming picture. She will soon sell
every one of her lovely bouquets!

The house is near a long road on
the edge of the village. See the mellow stone wall! See the dark rich
shutters and the comfortable seats
beside the door! Even the hardy vine
clinging to the wall lends its share of
color to the picture.

The road winds along one of the
narrow Dutch canals. The banks are
outlined by the pretty Dutch willows.

The road stretches far into the distance. See the dark color of the "near"

trees! They become lighter and lighter as they go back into the picture. The grass, too, is darker in the foreground. It grows lighter and softer as it goes back into the distance. This is one way in which the artist gives perspective to his painting.

Far down the road the sun glistens on a little white gate. The sun is very bright in Holland. Shining through the trees, it makes pretty lace-like patterns on the landscape.

See the dappled roadway! The soft, fleecy clouds above help to make the atmosphere warm and light. It is a long, long stretch of level green to the pretty light distance afar.

Our eyes travel easily along the road, and out into the distance. The artist has drawn the long vanishing lines of the road to lead us on and on. He has placed the trees in the very best position to carry us along. Though we see all over the picture, near and far, our eyes always come back to the flower girl. There she stands in her pretty white cap, violet dress, and blue-green apron, carrying her basket filled with the gayest of Holland flowers.

Though the artist has become famous for his many pictures of Holland, this is one of his best known paintings. It now hangs in the Art Institute of Chicago.

THE STORY OF THE ARTIST

George Hitchcock was among the first American artists to discover the beautiful light and color of Holland.

He saw the dazzling Holland sunlight! He saw the brilliance of tulip and hyacinth beds!

He saw beauty in the gay colored dresses, wooden shoes, and freshly starched caps of the Holland maidens.

The earlier painters of Dutch landscape had painted in tones of yellow and brown. The springtime brilliance of Holland had never been painted.

Though the sunshine of Holland had always been bright, though the flowers had always been gay, it had never occurred to these earlier painters to picture them so.

It was about forty-five years ago that a little group of artists studying in Holland began to catch the brilliance and glitter of sparkling sunlight. George Hitchcock was one of these.

"I could never make out," said he, "why artists should shun light and loveliness. There is light in Holland. There is beauty and charm. And the Dutch sunlight is not yellow, brown, or golden. Sunlight as I have discovered it is blue in tone. That is why I use so much blue and so much violet in my pictures."

George Hitchcock was born in Providence, Rhode Island, in 1850. His father had been known among his friends and neighbors as a painter. At this early date, however, the profession of painting was not highly regarded in the state of Rhode Island.

As a little fellow eight years old, George Hitchcock had begun to use the brush and paints. With great delight he covered page after page with glorious daubs of crimson, yellow, and blue! He would rather paint than do anything else! Little did he or his parents dream that this was the beginning of the masterpieces he would later weave in these same colors!

All through his school days he kept on painting. Though his parents were proud of his great ability, they felt the boy should go on with his studies, and then enter the business world.

Young Hitchcock felt so too. Instead of planning to be an artist, he decided to study law. Meanwhile he kept on with his painting.

He had graduated from Harvard University fully expecting to take up law, when he happened one day to be in Chicago. As he walked about, his attention was attracted by a sale of pictures by English artists. He stopped and looked over the paintings. Evidently he was not pleased, for as he turned away he said aloud to himself,—"I can do better than that myself."

That was the turning point in George Hitchcock's life! He began to paint!

He sold his pictures rapidly. He found that people liked his work. This greatly encouraged him. He resolved to give all his time to study. So law was given up, he packed his satchel, and started for Europe.

He studied in England for some time, and then crossed to Holland. This was one of the great events in his life. He found just what he had been looking for—sunlight and color.

There was the bright, glistening Holland sunshine!

There were the gay colored lilacs, hyacinths, and crocuses, such only as Holland knows!

To Mr. Hitchcock, Holland was filled

with sparkling color. This was not the Holland the older artists had painted. Their skies were yellow, brown, or gray. Oftentimes their peasants were dull and uninteresting. Oh, no! The older painters had not seen the gay tulips, hyacinths, and lilacs of Holland!

So delighted was this American artist with his new find, that he set to work immediately. He produced one picture after another.

One day the Empress of Austria happened to be in Holland. Fortunately she came upon one of Mr. Hitchcock's pictures. So pleased was she with the color and light of the painting, that she purchased it immediately. Soon after he began to carry off many honors and medals.

Reports of the artist's success began to come back to America. Soon painters on this side the water began to ask what "that Yankee Hitchcock was doing."

Then they flocked to Holland!

Suddenly the tulip fields of Holland became fashionable!

Mr. Hitchcock had always considered figure drawing an important part of an artist's education. He had given much study to this as well as to landscape. Now was his opportunity to combine the two in one picture. He painted the pretty Dutch maidens in their bright colored dresses. He pictured them walking through gay tulip fields, or along dappled country roads.

So delighted was Mr. Hitchcock with Holland, that this country became his adopted home. He lived there the greater part of his life, making only occasional visits to America. During the long summers he lived on his house-boat, which he had named "The Tulip." A part of the winters he spent in travel, but early spring always found him back amid the sparkling brilliance of the tulips and hyacinths of his beloved Holland.

DIRECTED STUDY

1. Where does the flower girl live?
   How do you know?
   For what is her country famous?

2. How is she dressed?
   How does she carry her flowers?
   What flowers do you think she carries?
   Name the colors in the flowers.
   Tell how the artist has placed them.
   From what direction does the light come?

3. What is the time of day? How do you know?
   What makes the pattern on the road?
   Name other places that reflect the sun.

4. What gives distance to the picture?
   Does the color of the trees help? How?

Does the size of the trees help?

Does the color of the grass help? How?

Does the edge of the brick walk help? How?

5. Describe the clouds and sky in the distance.

What "feeling" do they give the picture?

6. Who is the artist?

How are his pictures different from those of earlier painters?

Where is this picture?

Do you like it? Why?

Related Music: SPRING FLOWERS.....
............*Saint Saens*

ROSAMUNDE OVER-TURE ....*Schubert*

SPRING SONG.*Mendelssohn*

JEWELS OF THE MA-DONNA — First Inter-mezzo ......*Wolf-Ferrari*

VIEW OF GHENT
Brussels Gallery

ARTIST: Albert Baertsoen
SCHOOL: Belgian
DATES: 1866-1922

A VIEW OF GHENT

Ghent is one of the fascinating old cities of Belgium. It is modern in its new buildings, its electric tramways, and its business activity. One does not go far, however, before he is carried back to the dim distant past. Her quaint, steep-roofed houses, her narrow dark streets, her gloomy courtyards of medieval times, remind one constantly that Ghent is an old, old city.

The two rivers of Belgium, the Lys and the Scheldt, meet at the place where Ghent now stands. Here in the olden time, at the confluence of these rivers, a number of islands were formed. Upon one of these, somewhat higher and drier than the rest, the first house of Ghent was built. In the course of centuries, as the islands were gradually raised, other houses appeared. By and by the village spread from island to island, and little bridges were built to connect them. Gradually the town came to include twenty or thirty islands, joined by bridges. Then a wall and a deep moat were built surrounding the whole.

It is a street scene with one of these numerous little bridges that the artist pictures. See the stairs leading down to the canal below! See the steep sides of the embankment, and the boats lying at anchor! Above, this very stone bridge, no doubt, connects two little islands of Ghent.

This is an interesting time of the day for the painter. The sun is just going down. In fact it must be very close to the horizon, for the upper part of the picture is lighted, while the lower half is bathed in shadow. The light from the sinking sun strikes the red roofs and chimneys of these old houses of Ghent. How gay and picturesque they grow! The windows too, with few exceptions, gleam white in the reflected light.

This warm light in the upper part of the picture is a pleasing contrast to the cool gray of the street, and the shadows rising on the old walls. One can see that before long these gay houses will merge into gray.

The covered wagon and figures on the bridge become the darkest notes in the picture. These figures are no doubt clothed in dark materials, and being in the shadow take on still darker tones. These dark tones become the accents in the painting.

See how the artist leads into his picture! The long parallel lines of the railing catch the eye. They lead right on to the little bridge, to the covered wagon and the dark figures, then down the lighted street. The contrast of the dark wagon and figures against the light buildings makes this the "center of interest." Here, on the bridge, the artist has concentrated his darkest tones. Here the eye pauses.

The dark roofs and windows, to right

and left, take us all over the picture at a glance. Then if we like we may saunter down the little street, which doubtless leads, at the far end, to another little bridge.

Thus, you see, the artist has carefully considered his subject. He is not only painting a street scene in Ghent, but he is composing a picture. To do this he gives much thought to placing the scene on canvas. He thinks much of the lines leading into the picture; of the distribution of "darks" and "lights" over his canvas, and of the "center of interest." It is this that makes the picture-pattern. It is this that makes a work of art.

The artist who painted this picture knew all the little bridges, the narrow streets, the picturesque houses of Ghent. His sensitive eye selected many interesting street scenes, which he has painted with so much feeling, that he has become known as "the painter of street scenes."

THE STORY OF THE ARTIST

M. Albert Baertsoen, painter of the old cities of Belgium, was born in Ghent in 1866. He is one of the famous modern artists of Belgium. He is sometimes called the painter of "dead cities," because he wandered through these placid old towns of Flanders where life moves so slowly, painting the mouldering walls, ancient belfreys, old houses, and slow moving canals with their many-colored reflections.

He is an artist who seems to understand the spirit of these old towns, and while he paints the scenes as they appear, he is able to put into his picture much of his own "feeling" about them.

Baertsoen began to paint when he was quite young. Honors came to him quickly. Invariably he received recognition when exhibiting his pictures in the art centers of Paris, Berlin, Munich, and Brussels.

Baertsoen soon became known as a colorist. He seems to know the color of mouldering walls, of reflections in dreamy canals. He seems to know the secrets of color in the lights and shadows of a day most done. The color of the hour of dusk, just before nightfall, he catches as few others have done. In our picture, "A View of Ghent," it is this play of late sunlight which gives charm to the old street.

DIRECTED STUDY

1. Where is Ghent?
   How did it grow?
   How old is the city?

2. Describe the houses of Ghent.

3. What time of day is represented in the picture?
   How do you know?
   How does it affect the general scene?

4. How does the time of day affect the houses, windows, pavement?

5. Name the colors in the houses, roofs, chimneys.
   Name the colors in the pavement, railings, embankment.

6. How does the artist lead into the picture?
   Where is the "center of interest"?
   How is it accented?
   Where are these tones repeated?
   What effect does this have?
   What value does a picture-pattern give to a painting?

7. Who is the artist?
   Where was he born? When?
   What kind of pictures does he paint?
   For what is he especially noted?

Related Music: NOCTURNE E .....*Chopin*
　　　　　　　SOUVENIR ....*Drdla*

A DUTCH INTERIOR
Munich Gallery

ARTIST: Pieter de Hooch
SCHOOL: Dutch
DATES: 1629-1677

A DUTCH INTERIOR

Bright glowing sunshine! Soft mellow colors! Who have painted sunny interiors better than the painters of Holland?

The bright Holland sunshine delighted the Dutch artists, especially when it came streaming through pretty Dutch windows. They liked to paint the sharp patches of brilliant sunlight. They liked to paint the warm glowing shadows as they crept about the room. These Dutch artists painted light with so much skill, that after nearly three hundred years their pictures still glow.

This is, indeed, a pretty room! It has a low beamed ceiling, and beautiful, well-spaced windows. There is no great amount of furniture, but the artist has arranged it well. An old chest, two red chairs, two little red shoes, three little pictures with dark frames, and a woman reading a book, are the principal objects in the room.

How the sun shines in through the pretty Dutch windows! The lower part of the windows is darkened. This lets all the light in from above.

See the window-sash, golden-yellow! The woman sits in the full glow of the light. See, it shines upon her white bonnet and apron!

See the sharp reflection in the mirror! It leads down to the open book, then to the brilliant patches on the floor. It shines aslant on the side wall, cutting the corner of the red chair. It lights up the pretty red and yellow apples in the blue dish. It travels back again, across the room, to the white apron and bonnet of the reading woman.

How interested she is in her book! She wears a dark blue skirt and red sacque. She sits in a little straight-backed chair, and reads with the full sunlight upon the page.

Though the sunlight falls only in brilliant patches, the whole room is filled with light. Even the shadows glow. The walls are softened by the light moving upon them. Their yellow tints change to the yellowish browns of shadow, then into grays and greens, and by and by, in the deep corners, into dark notes. The floor catches the reflected lighted. The two dark framed pictures are illumined.

The artist carries the rich red over his picture in much the same way as the sunlight travels. It swings from the woman's red sacque to the red corner chair, then to the second red chair. Next, the little red shoes take up the color, which leads back again to the red sacque of the woman.

Notice how the little red shoes are placed! One is turned directly toward the reading figure. This helps the eye along, leading it straight to the Holland woman, interested only in her book.

Thus the rich red travels around the picture just as the sunlight does. This is the artist's way of composing color and light effects. When this composing is well done, a picture is called a *composition.*

With all this rich glowing color the artist found it necessary to have the dark pictures on the wall, and the dark mass in the lower left corner. These with the darkened lower windows serve as a balance of "dark" to the "light" in the room.

This interior is one of the famous masterpieces in Germany. Though it was painted nearly three hundred years ago, it is as bright and glowing as when it first came from the hand of the Dutch master. Today it hangs in the beautiful picture gallery at Munich.

THE STORY OF THE ARTIST

"Pieter de Hooch is a magician, and the sun is his wand." So said a French writer many years ago.

Yes! Pieter de Hooch is the painter of sunlight! It may be a simple Dutch interior; it may be a paved courtyard; it may be a red brick house with its garden and gate. But whatever it is, it is first of all bright glowing sunlight.

This artist loved rooms with high windows, and the sunlight streaming through. The open door, with a sunlit space beyond, was also a favorite. Dutch houses of red brick, aglow in sunlight, had an irresistible charm for him. Indeed, no one ever painted sunlight better than Pieter de Hooch!

Very little is known of this genius of the Netherlands. He was born in Rotterdam in 1630. Search where one may, however, not a word can be found about the little Dutch lad who grew up to be one of the greatest of Holland painters.

We do know, however, that after he was grown his life was spent in the various cities of Holland. Amsterdam and Delft are the two cities that claimed him most of the time.

At twenty-two he served as footman for a wealthy Hollander, and studied drawing and painting in his leisure moments. This gentleman was a patron of the arts, and probably encouraged the lad in his work.

At one time this wealthy Hollander sent his large collection of paintings to be sold. It contained ten pictures by Pieter de Hooch. These were valued in that day at from six to twenty florins each.* Today a single picture by this Dutch master is worth thousands of dollars!

Painting in Holland in this day was very different from what it was in Italy and England. There the painters were flourishing.

In Italy the churches made demands upon the artists for large paintings to cover the great expanse of wall surface. In England the king's court and the grand lords and ladies, in their

_____
*Florin; silver coin in value from 40c to 50c.

wonderful costumes of silks, velvets, and laces, were a constant inspiration to the painters.

Not so in Holland. Here the Dutch artists had to content themselves by painting little pictures of the everyday life of the Dutch people. The gay rollicking life of the Hollanders, their homes and their duties were the subjects to which they turned.

These painters of the little pictures of the Netherlands have become known as "Little Dutchmen."

Many of these "Little Dutchmen" are world-famed for their little pictures of the everyday life of the Dutch people. Among them is Pieter de Hooch, the painter of light, and of rich beautiful color. Though his pictures are small, each is a little gem in light and color.

De Hooch was a lover of glowing yellow and rich red. Every picture that he painted vibrates with these colors. The repetition of one bright color again and again over his picture is characteristic of his work. His love of rich beautiful red gained for him the name, "Red Pieter de Hooch."

His little Dutch rooms, Dutch houses, and Dutch courtyards are always aglow in the sunlight. Always the Dutch people are somewhere in his picture. Sometimes it is a Dutch mother and child; sometimes a cavalier; sometimes only a woman reading.

Though many of the famous Dutch painters of the day pictured the gay happy life of the Dutch people, this artist liked best to picture the home duties of the Dutch family. One picture he painted shows a mother teaching her little girl to lay away the clothes that have just been laundered. In another, a Dutch woman gives a little girl a pitcher of milk to carry home. In still another a little child is playing in the kitchen. It is always these simple scenes in the common life of the Hollander that de Hooch pictures.

It is interesting to know that the artist was never concerned about these people, who they were, or what they thought. He simply treated them as objects to make up his composition. They meant no more to him than a chair, a stool, or a bench. It was the color of their clothing, and their position in the picture that counted. He saw to it that they made an interesting note in his composition.

He thought light of far more importance than men, women, or children, and consequently gave it first place in his pictures.

People were never the actors in the pictures of de Hooch. The actor was the sunlight!

It streamed into the room. It danced on the floor. It played "hide and seek" about the objects in the room. It was always the bright, laughing sunshine that this artist painted!

It is the poetry of light in the pictures of de Hooch that has made his name immortal. These priceless little pictures of this famous Dutch painter now hang in the greatest galleries of the world.

DIRECTED STUDY

1. Where is this little room?
   How do you know?
   Do you like the windows? Why?

2. Where does the sunlight enter?
   What is its color?
   How does it travel around the picture?

3. Where is the brightest light?
   What is its color?
   Where are the deepest shadows?
   What is their color?
   How does the light affect the walls? Floors? Atmosphere?

4. What is the gayest color in the room?
   How does it travel around the picture?

5. Why did the artist place the shoes as he did?
   Describe the values of yellow. Of red.

6. Name the "darks" in the picture.
   Point out their arrangement.
   Does the light affect them?
   What is the "center of interest"?
   Name two ways in which it is emphasized.

7. What is a *composition?*
   How did the artist use figures?
   Name three excellent points in this composition.

8. Who is the artist?
   Where did he live? When?
   What nickname was given him? Why?
   What did he like best to paint?

Related Music: SPARKLETS . . . . *Moslowski*

THE FOG WARNING
Museum of Fine Arts, Boston

ARTIST: Winslow Homer
SCHOOL: American
DATES: 1836-1910

THE FOG WARNING

An approaching storm! The fog bells have sounded the warning! The cod-fisher hastens to the big fishing-boat for safety!

This is a frequent sight to those who live by the sea. Every morning the great fishing vessels, filled with sturdy fishermen, set sail for the day's work. They carry these hardy fisher folk far out to sea. After casting anchor in the deep, the men take to their flat-bottomed dories. Then each pulls off in a different direction.

All day long they try their fisherman's luck. Each is eager to bring in the biggest haul. Toward evening they return, unless perchance an unlooked-for storm or fog surprises them.

Our fisherman is out a long, long way on the rolling sea. In the distance a bank of heavy fog is rising. The great out-reaching arms mean danger, and the fisherman knows it. The sky is dark and gray. The sea reflects the leaden sky. It will soon be lashed into foam. Already the white-caps are beginning to play!

How cold, and hard, the deep blue-green of the sea! It rolls, and swishes, and surges, throwing its mist into the air.

The low wide dory is tilted for a moment in a deep trough of the sea. Ropes and anchor lie within. In the stern is a great white cod, its tail dashed against the gunwale of the boat. It is well that the fisherman has this extra load in his boat. He pauses as he looks back to locate the big fishing-boat in the distance. He is a sturdy old salt, but he prefers the safety of the old schooner in a storm like this.

Notice the way he holds the oars. See how their long lines repeat the sweep of the horizon, and fog-line in the distance. These long horizontal lines give a certain strength to the picture. We know this rugged fellow of the sea, with his long, hard pull, will reach haven.

The low wide dory, tipped aslant on the rolling waves, moves with the out-reaching arms of the distant fog bank. The swishing sea rolls hard about! The boat rises and falls. Movement is everywhere. The "smell of the sea" is in the air!

See how the artist draws attention to the forefront of the picture, then gradually leads back to the approaching cloud form. The pattern of the white cod against the dark boat, together with the light waves in the very front of the picture, catch the eye; next, we follow the fisherman's anxious gaze toward the white crest of the foaming wave, and on to the distant schooner.

See the pattern! From the great white cod to the white crest; to the schooner. Along the cloud bank to the tilted bow of the dory; the fisherman; and down again to the white cod! Constantly the eye travels round the pattern, taking in the whole of the picture. Such is the art of this master-painter!

THE STORY OF THE ARTIST

Winslow Homer knew the sea! Not only did he live for years on the rocky surf-beaten coast of Maine, but his people before him were sea-faring folk. Yes, the artist even claims a real pirate among his ancestors!

Winslow Homer was born in Boston, Massachusetts, in 1836. As a lad in school he early became known for his clever sketches and interesting drawings.

Winslow liked to draw. This was his greatest joy. About this time his father read an advertisement appearing in a Boston paper. BOY WANTED. MUST HAVE A TASTE FOR DRAWING. NO OTHER NEED APPLY. He decided that this was Winslow's opportunity. The work proved to be in a lithographer's shop. The young boy was taken into the shop. Here he worked steadily for two years. This was the small beginning of a career which led later to a place in the first rank of American painters.

After the lithographer's shop and study in a Boston art school came a position as illustrator for Harper's Weekly. During these years he occasionally painted pictures which brought him favorable notice and encouragement. All the pictures he may have painted in these early days, however, were of little consequence as compared with the great pictures of later years.

It was not until Winslow Homer heard "the call of the sea" that he became the great painter that he is. Going east to the rugged coast of Maine, he built his cabin up among the rocks. There from his window he looked out over the great expanse of sea.

Here the painter studied the calm.

Here he studied the storm. He knew the meaning of every cloud and every wind that blew.

Homer knew not only the sea, but the people who lived by the sea. He knew their work. He knew the dangers that threatened. He has pictured these men and women of the sea in all their rugged strength. His famous pictures, "All's Well," "The Life Line," and "Undertow" are paintings which show the familiar life of those who live by the sea.

Later he omitted these sturdy figures and painted only the grandeur and mystery of the sea.

Winslow Homer has painted the greatness and beauty of the sea, its overwhelming strength and majesty, as no other painter has ever done. He has painted the power of moving water, angry waves, and salt spray as few have done. For this reason he is recognized as America's foremost marine painter.

DIRECTED STUDY

1. Why does the fisherman hurry?
   How do you know he hurries?

2. What makes the movement in the picture?
   Suppose the dory were lengthwise with the horizon, would this give more or less movement?

3. Will the fisherman reach the boat?
   Why do you think so?

4. What is the color of the sea? Sky? Clouds? Boat? Shadow cast by the boat?
   What is the "center of interest"?

5. How is one led into the picture?
   Explain the picture-pattern.

6. Who is the artist?
   What qualities of the sea did he paint?
   How does he rank as a painter?

Related Music: STORM AT SEA........
................*Dürner*
THE STORM.......*Rossini*

JOAN OF ARC
Metropolitan Museum, New York

ARTIST: Jules Bastien-LePage
SCHOOL: French
DATES: 1848-1884

JOAN OF ARC

The life of Joan of Arc is one of the most amazing stories in the history of the world. A poor and unknown peasant girl leading the defeated, disheartened, and besieged forces of France to victory, seems an impossible legend. And yet this peasant girl of France did this very thing.

Joan lived in the little hamlet of France called Domremy. Here she toiled in the fields like other peasant children. When not in the fields she listened to her mother tell the stories of the saints, and the inspiring legends of her country.

When Joan was thirteen France was at war with England. Their last stronghold had just been besieged by the English. Naturally the people were despairing. The soldiers were deserting the army and all was gloom. Joan was moved to pity by the distress of her people. She thought and brooded over it. She prayed much about it.

One day she sat at her spinning wheel in the family garden. Suddenly a bright light shone round about. A vision of the archangel, St. Michael, appeared. Joan was so overcome that she fell to her knees. The angel announced that she, alone, must save France; that she, alone, must lead the armies of her beloved country to victory.

"But I am only a poor girl," she cried. "God will help you," replied the archangel.

Joan was so moved that she fell to weeping. She pondered the meaning of the strange visions over and over in her heart. Again and again the voices came, telling her to go to the aid of France.

Joan would reply: "I do not know how to ride, or lead men to arms." The reply was always the same: "Go. and the Lord be with you."

The poor child could have no peace

of mind. Finally, the villagers put their mites together and furnished her a horse. She rode off to see the prince.

When she arrived at the palace and told her story, the prince laughed her to scorn. Knowing, however, that his cause was well nigh lost, he finally decided to place Joan at the head of the French army. She was given white armor, and mounted upon a white charger. She was so inspiring a sight as she passed that all the people along the way first cheered, and then turned and knelt to pray. The troops were so inspired by her presence that victory was sure.

On she rushed to the very watch towers of the enemy. She carried in one hand the white standard of France, and in the other the unsheathed sword of St. Catherine.

Never had the English seen anything like it! After days of desperate fighting the siege was lifted. France was saved!

When later the prince was crowned King Charles VII, in the great cathedral at Rheims, Joan stood behind him, holding the standard of France.

One of the most beloved paintings in the Metropolitan Museum of New York City is this picture, "Joan of Arc," by Bastien-LePage.

In the midst of her father's garden stands this peasant maid, she who dreamed such dreams and saw such visions. She has been sitting at her spinning. Suddenly she hears the familiar voices. A strange light appears, and a figure in armor begins to form. Beside it, in the dimmest possible outlines, others are forming. Tradition says they are St. Michael, St. Catherine, and St. Margaret. Joan is thrilled. She rises. In her haste she overturns the stool.

There she stands, bewildered, trying to grasp the meaning of the strange words.

See the half-dazed expression of the

face! Her eyes are not the eyes of a dull, plodding peasant!

Perhaps she sees not only the beginning, but the end of her service as well!

Though Joan is a typical peasant—of strong build, heavy arms, large hands, broad neck, and firm chin—it is of little consequence. Though she wears the coarse clothes worn by all French peasants, they do not interest us. It is only the sad expression of the face, and the wondering half-dazed look of her eyes that awakens our sympathy.

Though there is much in the background—garden, cottage, trees, and "vision"—it is all well nigh lost. It serves only as a rich tapestry-like curtain which brings out, in strong relief, the figure of Joan. It is the face, and the face alone, that attracts and draws us again and again.

Before he made his great picture, the artist, Jules Bastien-LePage, made a special journey to Domremy to see the house where Joan lived. It is said that he set up his easel in the midst of the garden, and painted the scene as it was. Consequently this may be a very accurate picture of the house and garden. Though the trees and leaves somewhat hide the vision, we see it quite as plainly as did Joan.

The artist, too, has pictured Joan as the simple peasant maid that she was. Other artists have represented her as a saint, or a beautiful maiden astride a prancing horse. With so much feeling did our artist picture the vague, bewildered peasant face, that his picture immediately brought him fame.

The painting is signed by the artist himself, "J. Bastien-LePage, Damvillars Manse, 1879." It was purchased from the artist, and given to the Metropolitan Museum of Art, New York City, in 1889. It is a very large canvas, being eight feet four inches high, and nine feet three inches wide.

THE ARTIST

It is not surprising to know that the artist who painted "Joan of Arc" was born and reared in the Joan of Arc country. Damvillars is a little village not far from Domremy, where Joan had lived four hundred years before. The painter, Jules Bastien-LePage, was born in Damvillars in 1848.

From his earliest childhood he had been thrilled with the stirring adventures of this peasant maid of France. Little did he dream that he was destined to picture her story!

Jules was brought up in the country. His parents had planned to give the boy a general education sufficient to fit him for a worthy position in the city. When he was a mere child, however, he began to surprise his parents with his show of ability in drawing. The elder LePage was an artist of some merit, and took special delight in directing the boy's talent. During the long winter evenings he would set various objects on the table—books, a lamp, toys, and instruct the lad in drawing them. Though the parents were pleased at signs of this talent, they had no idea of their son becoming an artist.

When Jules was eleven years old he was sent to an academy in Verdun. He proved only an average student in his general studies. In no way did he distinguish himself except in his drawing classes. Here his ability was remarkable. His correctness in seeing, and his skill in drawing, won constant praise from his teachers.

The field of art opened a new world to him. Upon his return to his home, he informed his parents that he wanted to be an artist. This was a great shock to both his father and mother, as they had made other plans for the boy.

Fortunately, however, in the end the parents consented to the boy's wishes, and he was permitted to attend a famous art school in the city of Paris.

When he was twenty-five he won his first great success. He exhibited a portrait of his grandfather. This had been painted in an outdoor light. A picture in an outdoor light was something new at this time, and naturally created a great deal of interest and comment. From this time the public was interested in every picture that Bastien-LePage painted.

More and more the artists of the day were going out of doors to paint. It was this love of outdoor painting and truthful representation of nature that led Bastien-LePage to carry his easel and paints to the village of Domremy, to the very garden of Joan of Arc's home. Though he was always careful to paint nature exactly as she is, he possessed also the gift of imagination. The expression of Joan's face is a creation of artistic fancy.

This painting and others completed about this time were painted when

Bastien-LePage was at the very height of his power. He was then recognized as one of the great painters of France.

Just at this time, when still a young man, he suddenly became ill. Despite the efforts of friends and physicians alike, he passed away at the early age of thirty-seven years.

DIRECTED STUDY

1. Who was Joan of Arc?
   How many years ago did she live?
   Where did she live?
   How did she spend her time as a child?

2. What did she do for France?

3. What is the setting of this picture?
   Why has the artist placed Joan in this setting?

4. Who appears? What is the message?
   How does it affect Joan?

5. What is Joan's type?
   Describe her. Her dress.
   What is the most impressive feature
      of the painting?

6. What is the "center of interest"?
   How does the background empha-
      size the figure of Joan?
   What was the fate of Joan of Arc?
   Was her great service appreciated
      in her own day?
   Is it appreciated today?
   How do you know?

7. Who is the artist? Where did he
      live?
   What did he like best to paint?
   Does the picture show any imagina-
      tion? Where?
   Do you like it? Why?
   Where does the picture hang today?

Related Music: LARGO—New World Sym-
                    phony............*Dvorak*

JOAN OF ARC
Louvre, Paris

ARTIST: Henri Michel Antoine Chapu
SCHOOL: French
DATES: 1833-1891

JOAN OF ARC

Nearly five hundred years have passed since Joan of Arc was called to save France. It was in the little village of Domremy that she had heard the voices. It was here she had seen the visions that urged her on.

"Go, and the Lord be with you," were the words constantly ringing in her ears.

For the last four centuries the story of this little Maid of Orleans has appealed to painters and sculptors alike. Painters have represented her in picture. Sculptors have represented her in marble.

The painter, however, does not work like the sculptor. Neither does the sculptor work like the painter. The sculptor poses his figure in such a way that the figure, alone, is expressive of all he wishes to say. The painter, also, does this, but he may do more. He may add a background setting and other details to help tell the story.

In this beautiful single figure the sculptor tells the story of the "voices" quite as distinctly as any painter. Compare this statue with the famous painting, "Joan of Arc," by Bastien-LePage. Notice that each artist tells the same story, the one as a painter, the other as a sculptor.

The sculptor has told his story through the pose of one simple figure, while the painter added house, garden, and "vision" to carry his idea.

In the sculpture there is nothing without to suggest that Joan is hearing the heavenly voices, but we know it by the expression, not only of the face, but of the whole figure.

She is seated with hands tightly clasped. She gazes with uplifted eyes toward the vision. She hears the words, "Go, and the Lord be with you." In these words she reads her future. There is no turning away from this duty to which she has been called. The tenseness of the pose and the look in her eyes tell the whole story.

Again, she is the peasant maid, in the coarse dress of her type. The lines of the figure are somewhat softened, and not so heavy as in the painting by Bastien-LePage. Notice, too, that the peasant dress is especially adapted to sculpture. Its broad, simple surface becomes beautiful in marble. Further, the pose of the figure as a compact mass with no projecting parts, is a type best fitted to sculpture.

Notice the strong pull from hip to knee. This repeats the line of the arms, the lacing cord of the sacque, and its lower edge. This repetition of line helps to make the statue swing together. It gives unity to the composition. It produces beauty.

The figure appeals to the imagination. Its beauty lies in the *way* it has been composed, in its art, and not in its being a real statue of a real maiden.

For a long time this statue stood in the little village of Domremy, the French hamlet where Joan had lived for so many years. Later it was moved to the great gallery of the Louvre, in Paris, where it remains today.

Reproductions of this famous statue may be seen in many of the museums and art galleries of America.

Though Joan had led the French armies to victory, though she had saved France for the king, she suffered the death of a martyr. France has since, however, acknowledged her gratitude. In 1908 Joan was made a saint in the French calendar. She is now the beloved Saint Joan.

THE STORY OF THE SCULPTOR

It was about one hundred years ago that Henri Chapu, a little French boy, was born. This same little French boy grew up to be one of the famous modern sculptors of France.

When he was only a child he took great delight in making the plastic clay take all sorts of fantastic shapes. Later he studied modeling seriously. By and by his great genius as a sculptor was recognized not only by France, but by the whole world.

Like many other sculptors, he was fascinated by the story of the peasant maid of France. He modeled the figure of Joan of Arc just as he imagined it to be. When his statue was exhibited in Paris in 1870, the people praised both the statue and the sculptor. Though he has modeled many other figures, his statue of Joan of Arc is his best work.

This sculptor is known for the great simplicity of his compositions. His simple way of seeing the figures in marble is said to be the direct result of his study of Greek art. He took great pleasure in studying the beautiful marbles made by Greek sculptors who lived over two thousand years ago.

Many of these Greek marbles were carried away from Greece by victorious armies. Many were brought to western Europe. Today these same marbles are in the galleries of Europe.

Henri Chapu was so interested in Greek sculpture that he traveled through Europe studying in the art galleries and museums. He studied these figures so much that he soon began to work much as the Greek sculptors worked so many years ago.

His Joan of Arc has much of the simple grandeur of Greek sculpture.

DIRECTED STUDY

1. What is the difference between telling a story in marble, and telling it in color?

2. What story in the life of Joan does the artist tell?
   How do you know?

3. Describe the expression of Joan's face.

Describe the dress.

How does the dress add to the beauty of the sculpture?

4. Give one point about composition in marble that the artist has observed.

Point out the lines which create rhythm.

5. Do you like the statue? Why?

Which do you prefer,—the statue or the painting? Why?

6. Where was this statue first placed? Why?

Where is it today?

7. Who is the sculptor?

What is his native country?

What is one distinguishing characteristic of his work?

Related Music: ELEGIE ....*Massenet*
LA MARSEILLAIS ....
...............*De l'Isle*

CHRIST IN THE TEMPLE
Dresden Gallery

ARTIST: Heinrich Johann Hofmann
SCHOOL: German
DATES: 1824-1911

CHRIST IN THE TEMPLE

The great day had come! The young lad, Jesus, with his parents was soon to visit the holy city, Jerusalem. Ever since he had been a little child at his mother's knee, he had heard of the great day when he should see the wonderful city and temple. Now his dream was soon to be realized!

Jesus lived with his parents in the quiet village of Nazareth. They were pious Jewish people.

During Passover Week, it was the ambition of all Jewish people living in the country round about to make the annual visit to Jerusalem. Jerusalem was the holy city. Here upon the mount stood the beautiful temple. Within its sacred courts the learned doctors, rabbis, and scribes studied the Scriptures, and taught the people.

The Passover was the great yearly festival of the Jews; the temple was thronged with pilgrims, gathered in the holy city for this great occasion.

It was a beautiful day when the boy Jesus and his parents began their journey to Jerusalem. From all directions the pilgrims were gathering. The roads became more and more crowded, and as they drew near the city the throng grew greater. Soon, with songs of praise, they entered the city gates.

Day after day the pilgrims worshipped in the temple. Day after day they sat at the feet of the rabbis.

During one of these days toward the latter part of the week, Jesus stood among the pious Jews. He listened to the questions. He heard the replies of the learned rabbis.

He looked upon their wonderful robes. He observed their fine faces and thoughtful brows. He gave them reverence as teachers of the Sacred Law.

Soon they were touching upon deeper and more vital questions. He pushed forward and stood nearer. Suddenly he spoke. The doctors looked.

They listened. They were surprised to hear this little country lad speak with so much wisdom.

Soon they, in turn, began to question him. They asked about the Scriptures and their meaning. The answers were clear and sure. The doctors were astounded.

In the meantime the parents of the boy and others of the numerous bands of pilgrims were preparing to return to their homes. So many little companies were starting on their return journey that the narrow streets of the city were thronged. Pilgrims and donkeys everywhere!

The parents of Jesus, believing he was in their company, moved on with the others. Not until they had gone a day's journey did they miss the boy. Great was their grief and fear!

They hastened back to the city. They went to the temple. To their surprise and joy they found their son standing in the midst of the learned doctors, explaining to them the Scriptures. They were amazed.

Clad in a simple white tunic, the boy Jesus stands in their midst expounding to them the Law.

How quickly he catches our attention! Not only is he the center of the group, but all eyes, all thought is fixed upon him.

See the faces of those who listen! Each is interested. Each is different.

He is indeed a stern Pharisee who sits before the lad. The heavy book, which to him is the Law, rests upon his knees. He turns the pages. But the boy's wisdom astonishes him. He pauses to listen.

Next stands a younger man. Perhaps he is a scribe. He seems to have asked a puzzling question, and is listening to the lad's reply. His kindly face seems captivated by the boy's words.

The aged rabbi with the heavy white beard leans heavily with both hands upon his staff. He, too, listens. A whimsical smile plays over his features. He perhaps wonders how a little country boy from Nazareth could know so much. He is patient, however, and listens as the boy continues.

Leaning on the desk at the right is another stern Pharisee. See his eyes! See his face as he observes the boy! He holds the scroll of the Law firmly grasped in his hand. This to him is his faith.

Beyond, in the far corner, is still another listener. The wisdom of questions and answers has also caught his attention. He pauses to hear yet another word from the young lad in their midst.

See how the artist has suggested the temple, the learning of the East, and the richness of oriental color.

The two columns in the background and the reading-desk suggest that the group is within the temple. The open books and the parchment scroll give an air of learning and scholarship to the scene. The rich materials and inlaid chair lend magnificence to the picture.

See the rich robes of the doctors! Notice how the red of the Pharisee's robe is repeated, toned off, in the robes of the other figures. Notice how the gray-blue of the desk-cover and the robe of the leaning figure is repeated opposite in the headdress of the seated Pharisee. Thus the artist repeats his color over the picture, giving a color-pattern to the composition. Perhaps you observe the marked contrast between the richness of the Pharisee's robes and the simple white tunic of the boy.

Above all, however, is the illumined face of the child, and the interest in the faces of those who listen. The artist made these interesting faces shine out of the dark background by lighting the picture as he did. Notice how the full light falls upon the young lad, then upon the open book, then moves up to the face of the learned rabbi. It passes next to the young scribe; then to the older rabbi; across the picture to the face in the far left; then to the stern Pharisee in the foreground; and back again to the central figure. Thus, you see, the artist has arranged his light to make the eye travel all around the picture, and then lead back to the "center of interest." He has combined these many figures into one picture, largely by his arrangement of light. In this way the artist gives unity to his composition, and at the same time emphasizes the "center of interest."

The beautiful face of the lad is illumined with wisdom and aglow with gracious sympathy. It captivated these learned teachers of old. It has won the modern world as well. The radiance and charm of the face and figure of the Christ-child make this one of the most inspiring creations in modern art. No picture of modern times has met with greater public favor than has Hofmann's "Christ in the Temple."

THE STORY OF THE ARTIST

Heinrich Johann Hofmann is a German historical painter. He was born at Darmstadt in 1824. Later he moved to the beautiful city of Dresden, which became his home.

His many pictures based on Scripture stories have brought him fame. Among these, "Christ in the Temple" is most widely known.

Seldom is any picture placed in a great European gallery while the artist still lives. Herr Hofmann, however, is one of the few German artists who has enjoyed this distinction. He saw his picture, — "Christ in the Temple," placed with the masterpieces of the ages in the historic gallery of Dresden. Here he visited it many times.

It is said that the models for the Jewish types represented in the picture were found by the artist himself in the city of Dresden. These men were brought to the painter's studio. Here they posed as we see them in the picture.

Many have been the questions asked about the figure of the boy Jesus. So radiantly spiritual is the expression of the face that people have wondered where the artist could have found the model. Some said one thing; some said another. Finally it was reported that a young monk from a monastery in Spain had posed for the figure of the boy.

One day a student who happened to be in Dresden met the venerable painter. She ventured to ask him where he found the model for the boy Jesus.

"Found him?" he replied; "he was not found. I painted the boy just as I imagined him to look, just as I imagined him to be."

This from the artist himself settles forever the origin of the wonderful face. It is a creation of the artist's imagination.

This modern painter of Germany has

always been particularly friendly to American travelers. "Americans," he said, "appreciate my pictures." He told proudly of his picture,—"Christ in Gethsemane,"—that was purchased by an American, and later was the only object saved from his home in the great San Francisco fire.

Many Hofmann pictures have been reproduced in color, and are widely known. Today they are among the famous modern paintings of Germany.

DIRECTED STUDY

1. What story does this picture tell?
   Who are the men? Where are they?
   In whom are they interested?

2. What is the boy Jesus doing?
   To which of the doctors is he speaking?

3. What are the doctors doing?
   What thoughts do their faces show?

Are the expressions of faces alike?
Do you think they are more inter-
esting when alike, or unlike?
Why?
Which of the men would you like
best to know?

4. Why is the background indistinct?
How is the temple suggested?
How is learning suggested?
Name two colors and point out
where they have been repeated.
Why does the artist repeat his color?

5. What is the "center of interest"?
Point out three ways in which the
artist has emphasized this.
How has the artist combined his
figures into *one* picture?

6. Who is the artist?
Where did he find his models for
this picture?
Did he have a model for the child,
Jesus?
Where is the original picture?

Related Music: LARGO ....*Handel*

THE ANGELUS
Louvre, Paris

ARTIST: Jean Francois Millet
SCHOOL: French
DATES: 1814-1875

THE ANGELUS

The Angelus,—the vesper bell!
The day is done.
A silent prayer of gratitude ascends
For rest and peace.

The day is done. The low descending sun floods the field with its glowing light. The church bell in the distant tower sounds the vesper hour. The two peasants stand with bowed heads repeating the evening prayer.

Each morning, noon, and night the Angelus bell is heard in the hamlets of France. The ringing tones sweep far out over the fields. To all alike it carries the same message, a message of prayer.

The artist who painted this picture lived in a little village of France. From boyhood he had heard the Angelus bell. He knew its meaning well. It had made a deep impression on his sensitive mind. When he grew older he became one of the greatest artists of France. Then it was that he painted this picture of the peaceful evening hour, when only the sound of the Angelus is heard.

See the soft evening glow! It lights up the sky and field! It lights up the figure of the peasant woman. It makes bright patches on her apron, sleeve, and wooden shoes. Her head is bowed. See the silhouette made by her head and shoulders against the evening sky! It is well that the apron is light, for in catching the fading glow, it accents her figure, making it of far greater interest.

Opposite, with head bowed, and hat in hand, stands her companion. He stands with his back to the light. This makes his figure a silhouette relieved against the light sky and field. His clothes are of coarse material and dark in color. Only a glimpse of the light shirt is seen, repeating the light in the woman's apron. Nearby, the long handle of the fork placed upright in the ground, repeats the line of the two figures. The wheelbarrow with its load, and the basket full to the brim, rest beside the furrow. Both these workers, with their wheelbarrow and basket, will soon begin the long walk over the field to the village.

It is a long, long walk to the village! The artist has placed the skyline high. This gives a field reaching far to the distant horizon. Here the sky melts into a hazy golden light. The middle distance, stretching across the picture, reflects the yellow glow. These broad horizontal effects of middle distance, horizon, and expanse of sky give quiet and repose to the picture. Thus, you see, the artist has created a background in keeping with the mood of the painting.

The foreground alone is dark in color. Here, at the close of the day, stand these patient workers. In the sacred hush of the Angelus hour, they pause and bow in prayer.

How different if the heads had been raised! How this would change the picture! The bowed head against the evening sky is the very heart of the painting. This gives the keynote to the picture. This suggests the feeling of reverence. This breathes the benediction of the Angelus hour.

As a child the artist had been deeply impressed by the Angelus bell. One day he went with his mother to see new bells fitted into the church tower. He was amazed at their size, and when they were struck, he marveled at the deep resounding tone. Later he said that, in this painting, he wanted to make everyone "hear the deep tones of the Angelus bell."

As one quietly contemplates the picture, and enters into the mood of the artist, he, too, may hear the deep tones of the Angelus. His thought, too, may unite with that of these humble workers in the gentle reverence of this tranquil, twilight hour.

THE STORY OF THE ARTIST

Jean Francois Millet has passed into history as "the peasant-painter of France." This painter of peasants was himself a farmer lad. He was born on a farm in the north of France in 1814.

Here in this wide open country he grew up. Here his young mind was stored with visions of distant horizons, vast fields, and busy workers.

Though the family was classed as peasants, today they would be considered more as independent farmers; for they owned their land and the Millet family had tilled it for centuries. It had been handed down from father to son through a long line of ancestors.

From these ancestors, moreover, they had inherited something which they prized more highly than land. That was a grand good name, a name which stood for integrity, industry, and piety. As far back as was possible to remember, the family, Millet, had been known for its fine sterling worth.

Jean was the eldest of eight children. As a child he worked with his brothers and sisters in the fields. One day he surprised them by making little sketches of sheep. Another time he modeled these same sheep in soft clay which he found on the farm. By and by he was sketching the cattle and geese about the farm, and the figures of peasant workers.

As he grew older he continued to surprise the family with his many sketches and models in clay. One day when he and his father were returning from church, they passed an old man, stoop-shouldered and gray. Upon reaching home the lad sketched the figure with charcoal upon the wall. So remarkable was the drawing that the man was recognized immediately. This was the turning point in the boy's life. The father decided that his talent must be developed.

Accordingly he was sent to Cherburg, a near-by city, for instruction. He remained there for three years. The artists were so astonished at his ability that no one wanted to teach him. Later he went to Paris to continue his studies.

Paris had always been a dream city to the boy. Now, indeed, he beheld it in reality. The great city with its throbbing life was a wonderful world to him. One of the first visits he made was to the great picture gallery of the Louvre. Here, he said, his feelings were "too great for words." Then he added: "I closed my eyes lest I be dazzled by the sight, and dared not open them lest I should find it all a dream."

Here, in Paris, Millet began his long struggle for recognition. His ideas of painting and picture-making were very different from those of the leading artists of Paris. He painted life as he saw it—the busy workers in the fields, the hard working peasants. No one had ever seen such subjects in a picture before. The public did not like pictures of working people. Naturally they thought Millet peculiar, eccentric, and not much of a painter, after all.

Millet worked for twelve long years in Paris. He struggled along as best he could to make a living. Painting portraits, landscapes, and even signs for the tailor and sail-maker, he eked out a pathetic existence. Paris seemed to hold nothing for him. He longed for the open fields, and the simple life of his childhood. He resolved to escape from the city into the country, and follow out his own ideas in painting.

About a day's ride from Paris brings one to the little village of Barbizon. Here were the wide fields and the quiet life for which the artist longed. This he decided to make his future home.

Here, surrounded by a wide stretch of open country, and living in the midst of the people he loved, he painted the pictures which today are among the great pictures of the world.

It was only during the last few years

of his life that Millet won recognition and was well paid for his work.

It was here in 1859 that he completed his now celebrated painting,—"The Angelus." That same year it was sold for approximately $400. Later it was sold and resold for constantly increasing prices. Once when it changed hands for $10,000, Millet thought this an enormous sum. He was very apologetic, and assured his friends that he had nothing to do with the transaction. Later, many years after the painter's death, in its final sale "The Angelus" brought over $150,000. It now hangs in the beautiful gallery of the Louvre.

After Millet had won recognition his friends came from the great outside world to see him at Barbizon. These friends were the artists, scholars, and men of letters from the great cities. Though he was recognized far and wide, and received many honors, he preferred above all else his simple quiet life in Barbizon.

DIRECTED STUDY

1. What is the Angelus?
   When did it ring? Why?

2. What time of day is represented?
   Where is the sun? How do you
   know?

3. What is the general tone of the
   picture?
   Where is the light brightest? Why?

4. Who are these people? Where do
   they live?
   Describe their type.
   Which is the more important?
   How has the artist shown this?

5. What is the main thought of the
   picture?
   Point out one part of the composition that gives the keynote of
   feeling to the picture.

6. How much of the picture is sky?
   Ground?
   How far back is the village?

7. How does the artist give a feeling
   for space back of the figure?
   How does he give repose and quiet
   to the scene?
   Does this fit the mood of the picture?

8. Why did the artist place the fork as
   he did? Why does it lean?
   What adds a note of balance?

9. Who is the artist?
   What kind of pictures did he paint?
   How does he rank as a painter
   today?
   For what did the Angelus first sell?
   What is its value now?

Related Music: THE ANGELUS ..*Massenet*

AVE MARIA .....*Schubert*

EVENING BELLS ......
.................*Abt.*

PRONUNCIATION OF PROPER NAMES

BAERTSOEN ...... (baẽrt′ sōn)

BASTIEN-LEPAGE, JULES...
..... (zhōōl bas′ tyăn′ lĕ päzh′)

COURRIERES....... (kö′ rĭ′ är′)

DOMREMY.......... (dō′ rā′ mī′)

DAMVILLARS... (dähn′ vēēl′ är′)

CHAPU, HENRI ....
(ähn′ rĭ′ chä′ poo′, OO as in TOO)

DE HOOCH.......... (dā hōk′)

HALS .... (hälz)

MILLET, JEAN FRANCOIS...
...... (zhän frän′ swä′ mē′ yā′)

RUYSDAEL .... (rois′ däl)

GHENT.... (gĕnt, G as in GET)

HOFMANN, HEINRICH
JOHANN ....
... (hīn′ rĭch yō′ hän hōf′ man)

LYS .... (lĭ′ e)

RHEIMS.... (rēmz. French, răńs)

SCHELDT .... (skĕlt)

SÈVRES .... (sâ′ vr)

SUGGESTIONS TO TEACHERS

STUDYING THE PICTURE. Any picture presented for study becomes more interesting when freely discussed in a natural way by the class. Before reading the text it is always advisable to study the picture. Pupils should be encouraged to give their own impressions; tell what they like in a picture; and WHY they like it.

In the intermediate and grammar grades simple elements in picture-making may be pointed out,—i.e. light and shade, repetition of line, of color, color harmony, balance, and center of interest. Such questions as,—From what direction does the light come? Where does it shine brightest?—and others of a similar nature, may help the pupil to SEE. Led by the teacher's skillful questioning, pupils gradually acquire the ability to discover for themselves many elements of design in picture-making.

DRAMATIZATION. Many of the pictures used in the intermediate and grammar grades lend themselves to dramatization. Under no circumstances is it necessary to burden one's self, in the class room, with an exact reproduction. The details of costume are not required. Any outstanding accessory of dress, easily at hand, may, however, add interest. It is the pose of the figure, the grouping if there are several, and the action, that are best appreciated by the pupils when the effort is made to reproduce a picture.

CORRELATION. Many of the famous pictures of this series bear directly upon interesting historical events. These, in particular, furnish subjects for language and composition.

Drawing lessons may with real profit be given over to the tracing of pictures, for the purpose of studying line, composition, light, and shade.

The music hour offers still another

opportunity for related study. Pictures, like music, create emotions. When possible in the study of pictures, add the music which suggests the spirit and atmosphere of the picture. THE INTEREST IS ALWAYS KEENLY STIMULATED WHEN PORTIONS FROM VARIOUS SELECTIONS ARE PLAYED, AND THE CHILDREN PERMITTED TO CHOOSE THE ONE BEST SUITED TO THE PICTURE.

The suggestions for musical selections, which follow the questions on the picture, will be of great value to the teacher.

As far as possible, each pupil should own his own pictures. This leads to the making of picture-study books, envelopes, and folders, for preserving his pictures.

STUDY OF ARTISTS. Many times when studying an artist, children are delighted to bring to the class room other reproductions of his pictures.

This always stimulates interest. With several pictures by the same artist before the class, the outstanding characteristics of the painter, whether in color, composition, or some other phase of picture-making, may be intelligently discussed by the pupils. After such study as this, what "Millet" or "Rembrandt" will not be instantly recognized!

Sometimes pictures of the same subject by different artists are an equally interesting form of study. Such a series under a general subject, — as "Knighthood," "Trees," "Boats," "Joan of Arc"—affords many opportunities for valuable comparisons. Children will readily discover that each of the artists, treating the same subject, tells his story in a different way. This cultivates intelligent SEEING, and appreciation.

Free discussion of pictures before the class are always vital to real enjoyment of the masterpieces.

To be introduced in early years to the masterpieces of the ages, and to learn of the kingly minds who have ruled in this realm of beauty, is sure to develop an interest which will enlarge, enrich, and refine the future life of the pupil.

www.ingramcontent.com/pod-product-compliance
Lightning Source LLC
Chambersburg PA
CBHW041719090426
42739CB00018B/3474